52nd Annual Meeting of the Association for Computational Linguistics (ACL 2014)

Tutorial Abstracts

Baltimore, Maryland, USA
22 June 2014

ISBN: 978-1-63439-194-8

Printed from e-media with permission by:

Curran Associates, Inc.
57 Morehouse Lane
Red Hook, NY 12571

Some format issues inherent in the e-media version may also appear in this print version.

Printed by Curran Associates, Inc. (2014)

For permission requests, please contact the Association for Computational Linguistics at the address below.

Association for Computational Linguistics
209 N. Eighth Street
Stroudsburg, Pennsylvania 18360

Phone: 1-570-476-8006
Fax: 1-570-476-0860

acl@aclweb.org

Additional copies of this publication are available from:

Curran Associates, Inc.
57 Morehouse Lane
Red Hook, NY 12571 USA
Phone: 845-758-0400
Fax: 845-758-2634
Email: curran@proceedings.com
Web: www.proceedings.com

ACL 2014

52nd Annual Meeting of the Association for Computational Linguistics

Proceedings of the Conference Tutorial Abstracts

22 June 2014
Baltimore, Maryland, USA

Introduction

This volume contains the abstracts of the ACL 2014 tutorials. We received 19 high-quality proposals, and it was a difficult task to make a final selection. We applied the following criteria for evaluation: appropriateness, technical fit, novelty, potential interest, presenters, and experience. In the end we accepted eight tutorials. All eight of these are organized as half-day tutorials.

We are very grateful to David Yarowsky (local chair), Alexander Koller and Yusuke Miyao (publication chairs), Daniel Marcu (general chair), Johan Bos and Keith Hall (the ACL 2013 tutorial chairs), and of course Priscilla Rasmussen, for various kinds of help, advice and assistance offered during the process of putting the tutorial programme and materials together. Most importantly, we would like to thank the tutorial presenters for the time and effort in preparing and presenting the tutorials.

We hope you will enjoy the tutorials!

ACL 2014 Tutorial Chairs
Alex Fraser (CIS, University of Munich)
Yang Liu (Tsinghua University)

Organizers:

Alex Fraser (CIS, University of Munich)
Yang Liu (Tsinghua University)

Table of Contents

Conference Program

June 22, 2014

Morning

9:00–12:30 *Gaussian Processes for Natural Language Processing*
Trevor Cohn, Daniel Preotiuc-Pietro and Neil Lawrence

9:00–12:30 *Scalable Large-Margin Structured Learning: Theory and Algorithms*
Liang Huang, Kai Zhao and Lemao Liu

9:00–12:30 *Semantics for Large-Scale Multimedia: New Challenges for NLP*
Florian Metze and Koichi Shinoda

9:00–12:30 *Wikification and Beyond: The Challenges of Entity and Concept Grounding*
Dan Roth, Heng Ji, Ming-Wei Chang and Taylor Cassidy

Afternoon

14:00–17:30 *New Directions in Vector Space Models of Meaning*
Phil Blunsom, Georgiana Dinu, Edward Grefenstette and Karl Moritz Hermann

14:00–17:30 *Structured Belief Propagation for NLP*
Matthew Gormley and Jason Eisner

14:00–17:30 *Semantics, Discourse and Statistical Machine Translation*
Deyi Xiong and Min Zhang

14:00–17:30 *Syntactic Processing Using Global Discriminative Learning and Beam-Search Decoding*
Yue Zhang, Meishan Zhang and Ting Liu

Gaussian Processes for Natural Language Processing

Trevor Cohn
Computing and Information Systems
The University of Melbourne
trevor.cohn@gmail.com

Daniel Preoţiuc-Pietro and **Neil Lawrence**
Department of Computer Science
The University of Sheffield
{daniel,n.lawrence}@dcs.shef.ac.uk

1 Introduction

Gaussian Processes (GPs) are a powerful modelling framework incorporating kernels and Bayesian inference, and are recognised as state-of-the-art for many machine learning tasks. Despite this, GPs have seen few applications in natural language processing (notwithstanding several recent papers by the authors). We argue that the GP framework offers many benefits over commonly used machine learning frameworks, such as linear models (logistic regression, least squares regression) and support vector machines. Moreover, GPs are extremely flexible and can be incorporated into larger graphical models, forming an important additional tool for probabilistic inference. Notably, GPs are one of the few models which support analytic Bayesian inference, avoiding the many approximation errors that plague approximate inference techniques in common use for Bayesian models (e.g. MCMC, variational Bayes).[1] GPs accurately model not just the underlying task, but also the uncertainty in the predictions, such that uncertainty can be propagated through pipelines of probabilistic components. Overall, GPs provide an elegant, flexible and simple means of probabilistic inference and are well overdue for consideration of the NLP community.

This tutorial will focus primarily on regression and classification, both fundamental techniques of wide-spread use in the NLP community. Within NLP, linear models are near ubiquitous, because they provide good results for many tasks, support efficient inference (including dynamic programming in structured prediction) and support simple parameter interpretation. However, linear models are inherently limited in the types of relationships between variables they can model. Often non-linear methods are required for better understanding and improved performance. Currently, kernel methods such as Support Vector Machines (SVM) represent a popular choice for non-linear modelling. These suffer from lack of interoperability with down-stream processing as part of a larger model, and inflexibility in terms of parameterisation and associated high cost of hyperparameter optimisation. GPs appear similar to SVMs, in that they incorporate kernels, however their probabilistic formulation allows for much wider applicability in larger graphical models. Moreover, several properties of Gaussian distributions (closure under integration and Gaussian-Gaussian conjugacy) means that GP (regression) supports analytic formulations for the posterior and predictive inference.

This tutorial will cover the basic motivation, ideas and theory of Gaussian Processes and several applications to natural language processing tasks. GPs have been actively researched since the early 2000s, and are now reaching maturity: the fundamental theory and practice is well understood, and now research is focused into their applications, and improve inference algorithms, e.g., for scaling inference to large and high-dimensional datasets. Several open-source packages (e.g. GPy and GPML) have been developed which allow for GPs to be easily used for many applications. This tutorial aims to promote GPs, emphasising their potential for widespread application across many NLP tasks.

2 Overview

Our goal is to present the main ideas and theory behind Gaussian Processes in order to increase awareness within the NLP community. The first part of the tutorial will focus on the basics of Gaussian Processes in the context of regression. The Gaussian Process defines a prior over functions which applied at each input point gives a response

[1] This holds for GP regression, but note that approximate inference is needed for non-Gaussian likelihoods.

value. Given data, we can analytically infer the posterior distribution of these functions assuming Gaussian noise.

This tutorial will contrast two main applications settings for regression: interpolation and extrapolation. Interpolation suits the use of simple radial basis function kernels which bias towards smooth latent functions. For extrapolation, however, the choice of the kernel is paramount, encoding our prior belief about the type of function wish to learn. We present several different kernels, including non-stationary and kernels for structured data (string and tree kernels). One of the main issues for kernel methods is setting the hyperparameters, which is often done in the support vector literature using grid search on held-out validation data. In the GP framework, we can compute the probability of the data given the model which involves the integral over the parameter space. This marginal likelihood or *Bayesian evidence* can be used for model selection using only training data, where by model selection we refer either to choosing from a set of given covariance kernels or choosing from different model hyperparameters (kernel parameters). We will present the key algorithms for type-II maximum likelihood estimation with respect to the hyper-parameters, using gradient ascent on the marginal likelihood.

Many problems in NLP involve learning from a range of different tasks. We present multi-task learning models by representing intra-task transfer simply and explicitly as a part of a parameterised kernel function. GPs are an extremely flexible probabilistic framework and have been successfully adapted for multi-task learning, by modelling multiple correlated output variables (Alvarez et al., 2011). This literature develops early work from geostatistics (*kriging* and *co-kriging*), on learning latent continuous spatio-temporal models from sparse point measurements, a problem setting that has clear parallels to transfer learning (including domain adaptation).

In the application section, we start by presenting an open-source software package for GP modelling in Python: GPy.[2] The first application we approach the regression task of predicting user influence on Twitter based on a range or profile and word features (Lampos et al., 2014). We exemplify how to identifying which features are best for predicting user impact by optimising the hyperparameters (e.g. RBF kernel length-scales) using Automatic Relevance Determination (ARD). This basically gives a ranking in importance of the features, allowing interpretability of the models. Switching to a multi-task regression setting, we present an application to Machine Translation Quality Estimation. Our method shows large improvements over previous state-of-the-art (Cohn and Specia, 2013). Concepts in automatic kernel selection are exemplified in an extrapolation regression setting, where we model word time series in Social Media using different kernels (Preoţiuc-Pietro and Cohn, 2013). The Bayesian evidence helps to select the most suitable kernel, thus giving an implicit classification of time series.

In the final section of the tutorial we give a brief overview of advanced topics in the field of GPs. First, we look at non-conjugate likelihoods for modelling classification, count and rank data. This is harder than regression, as Bayesian posterior inference can no longer be solved analytically. We will outline strategies for non-conjugate inference, such as expectation propagation and the Laplace approximation. Second, we will outline recent work on scaling GPs to big data using variational inference to induce sparse kernel matrices (Hensman et al., 2013). Finally – time permitting – we will finish with unsupervised learning in GPs using the latent variable model (Lawrence, 2004), a non-linear Bayesian analogue of principle component analysis.

3 Outline

1. GP Regression (60 mins)
   (a) Weight space view
   (b) Function space view
   (c) Kernels
2. NLP Applications (60 mins)
   (a) Sparse GPs: Predicting user impact
   (b) Multi-output GPs: Modelling multi-annotator data
   (c) Model selection: Identifying temporal patterns in word frequencies
3. Further topics (45 mins)
   (a) Non-congjugate likelihoods: classification, counts and ranking
   (b) Scaling GPs to big data: Sparse GPs and stochastic variational inference

[2] `http://github.com/SheffieldML/GPy`

(c) Unsupervised inference with the GP-LVM

4 Instructors

Trevor Cohn[3] is a Senior Lecturer and ARC Future Fellow at the University of Melbourne. His research deals with probabilistic machine learning models, particularly structured prediction and non-parametric Bayesian models. He has recently published several seminal papers on Gaussian Process models for NLP with applications ranging from translation evaluation to temporal dynamics in social media.

Daniel Preoţiuc-Pietro[4] is a final year PhD student in Natural Language Processing at the University of Sheffield. His research deals with applying Machine Learning models to model large volumes of data, mostly coming from Social Media. Applications include forecasting future behaviours of text, users or real world quantities (e.g. political voting intention), user geo-location and impact.

Neil Lawrence[5] is a Professor at the University of Sheffield. He is one of the foremost experts on Gaussian Processes and non-parametric Bayesian inference, with a long history of publications and innovations in the field, including their application to multi-output scenarios, unsupervised learning, deep networks and scaling to big data. He has been programme chair for top machine learning conferences (NIPS, AISTATS), and has run several past tutorials on Gaussian Processes.

References

Mauricio A. Alvarez, Lorenzo Rosasco, and Neil D. Lawrence. 2011. Kernels for vector-valued functions: A review. *Foundations and Trends in Machine Learning*, 4(3):195–266.

Trevor Cohn and Lucia Specia. 2013. Modelling annotator bias with multi-task Gaussian processes: an application to machine translation quality estimation. In *Proceedings of the 51st annual meeting of the Association for Computational Linguistics*, ACL.

James Hensman, Nicolo Fusi, and Neil D. Lawrence. 2013. Gaussian processes for big data. In *Proceedings of the 29th Conference on Uncertainty in Artificial Intelligence*, UAI.

Vasileios Lampos, Nikolaos Aletras, Daniel Preoţiuc-Pietro, and Trevor Cohn. 2014. Predicting and characterising user impact on Twitter. In *Proceedings of the 14th Conference of the European Chapter of the Association for Computational Linguistics*, EACL.

Neil D. Lawrence. 2004. Gaussian process latent variable models for visualisation of high dimensional data. *NIPS*, 16(329-336):3.

Daniel Preoţiuc-Pietro and Trevor Cohn. 2013. A temporal model of text periodicities using Gaussian Processes. In *Proceedings of the Conference on Empirical Methods in Natural Language Processing*, EMNLP.

Kashif Shah, Trevor Cohn, and Lucia Specia. 2013. An investigation on the effectiveness of features for translation quality estimation. In *Proceedings of the Machine Translation Summit*.

[3]http://staffwww.dcs.shef.ac.uk/people/T.Cohn

[4]http://www.preotiuc.ro

[5]http://staffwww.dcs.shef.ac.uk/people/N.Lawrence

Scalable Large-Margin Structured Learning: Theory and Algorithms

Liang Huang **Kai Zhao** **Lemao Liu**
Graduate Center and Queens College, City University of New York
{liang.huang.sh, kzhao.hf, lemaoliu}@gmail.com

1 Motivations

Much of NLP tries to map structured input (sentences) to some form of structured output (tag sequences, parse trees, semantic graphs, or translated/paraphrased/compressed sentences). Thus structured prediction and its learning algorithm are of central importance to us NLP researchers. However, when applying machine learning to structured domains, we often face scalability issues for two reasons:

1. Even the fastest exact search algorithms for most NLP problems (such as parsing and translation) is too slow for repeated use on the training data, but approximate search (such as beam search) unfortunately breaks down the nice theoretical properties (such as convergence) of existing machine learning algorithms.
2. Even with inexact search, the scale of the training data in NLP still makes pure online learning (such as perceptron and MIRA) too slow on a single CPU.

This tutorial reviews recent advances that address these two challenges. In particular, we will cover principled machine learning methods that are designed to work under vastly inexact search, and parallelization algorithms that speed up learning on multiple CPUs. We will also extend structured learning to the latent variable setting, where in many NLP applications such as translation and semantic parsing the gold-standard derivation is hidden.

2 Contents

1. Overview of Structured Learning
   (a) key challenge 1: search efficiency
   (b) key challenge 2: interactions between search and learning
2. Structured Perceptron
   (a) the basic algorithm
   (b) the geometry of convergence proof
   (c) voted and averaged perceptrons, and efficient implementation tricks
   (d) applications in tagging, parsing, etc.
3. Structured Perceptron under Inexact Search
   (a) convergence theory breaks under inexact search
   (b) early update
   (c) violation-fixing perceptron
   (d) applications in tagging, parsing, etc.

   —coffee break—

4. From Perceptron to MIRA
   (a) 1-best MIRA; geometric solution
   (b) k-best MIRA; hildreth algorithm
   (c) MIRA with all constraints; loss-augmented decoding
   (d) MIRA under inexact search
5. Large-Margin Structured Learning with Latent Variables
   (a) examples: machine translation, semantic parsing, transliteration
   (b) separability condition and convergence proof
   (c) latent-variable perceptron under inexact search
   (d) applications in machine translation
6. Parallelizing Large-Margin Structured Learning
   (a) iterative parameter mixing (IPM)
   (b) minibatch perceptron and MIRA

3 Instructor Biographies

Liang Huang is an Assistant Professor at the City University of New York (CUNY). He received his Ph.D. in 2008 from Penn and has worked as a Research Scientist at Google and a Research Assistant Professor at USC/ISI. His work is mainly on the theoretical aspects (algorithms and formalisms) of computational linguistics, as well as theory and algorithms of structured learning. He has received a Best Paper Award at ACL 2008, several best paper nominations (ACL 2007, EMNLP 2008, and ACL 2010), two Google Faculty Research Awards (2010 and 2013), and a University Graduate Teaching Prize at Penn (2005). He has given two tutorials at COLING 2008 and NAACL 2009, being the most popular tutorial at both venues.

Kai Zhao is a Ph.D. candidate at the City University of New York (CUNY), working with Liang Huang. He received his B.S. from the University of Science and Technology in China (USTC). He has published on structured prediction, online learning, machine translation, and parsing algorithms. He was a summer intern with IBM TJ Watson Research Center in 2013.

Lemao Liu is a postdoctoral research associate at the City University of New York (CUNY), working with Liang Huang. He received his Ph.D. from the Harbin Institute of Technology in 2013. Much of his Ph.D. work was done while visiting NICT, Japan, under Taro Watanabe. His research area is machine translation and machine learning.

Semantics for Large-Scale Multimedia: New Challenges for NLP

Florian Metze
Carnegie Mellon University
fmetze@cs.cmu.edu

Koichi Shinoda
Tokyo Institute of Technology
shinoda@cs.titech.ac.jp

1 Description

Thousands of videos are constantly being uploaded to the web, creating a vast resource, and an ever-growing demand for methods to make them easier to retrieve, search, and index. As it becomes feasible to extract both low-level as well as high-level (symbolic) audio, speech, and video features from this data, these need to be processed further, in order to learn and extract meaningful relations between these. The language processing community has made huge process in analyzing the vast amounts of very noisy text data that is available on the Internet. While it is very difficult to create semantic units of low-level image descriptors or non-speech sounds by themselves, it is comparatively easy to ground semantics in the word output of a speech recognizer, or text data that is loosely associated with a video. This creates an opportunity for NLP researchers to use their unique skills, and make significant contributions to solve tasks on data that is even noisier than web text, but (we argue) even more interesting and challenging.

This tutorial aims to present to the NLP community the state of the art in audio and video processing, by discussing the most relevant tasks at NIST's TREC Video Retrieval Evaluation (TRECVID) workshop series. We liken "Semantic Indexing" (SIN) task, in which a system must identify occurrences of concepts such as "desk", or "dancing" in a video to the word spotting approach. We then proceed to explain more recent, and challenging tasks, "Multimedia Event Detection" (MED) and "Multimedia Event Recounting" (MER), which can be compared to transcription and summarization tasks. Finally, we will present an easy way to get started in multi-media analysis using Virtual Machines from the "Speech Recognition Virtual Kitchen", which will enable tutorial participants to perform hands-on experiments during the tutorial, and at home.

2 Outline

1. Introduction
    - Content based video retrieval
    - What is the "Semantic Gap"?
    - The TRECVid workshop and its tasks
2. Semantic Indexing
    - State-of-the art frameworks
    - Extension of Bag-of-Word model
    - Multi-modality
3. Multimedia Event Detection & Recounting
    - State-of-the art frameworks
    - Multimodal fusion
    - Semi-supervised and active learning
    - Video Summarization
4. Challenges for NLP
    - How to design visual concepts?
    - Intermediate representations?
    - Are there any grammars in video?
5. Practice session
    - Virtual Machines in the Speech Recognition Virtual Kitchen (http://speechkitchen.org/)

3 Instructors

Florian Metze received his PhD from Universitat Karlsruhe (TH) in 2005. He worked as a Senior Research Scientist at Deutsche Telekom Laboratories (T-Labs) and joined Carnegie Mellon University's faculty in 2009. His interests includes speech and audio processing, and user interfaces.
Koichi Shinoda received his D. Eng. from Tokyo Institute of Technology in 2001. In 1989, he joined NEC Corporation. From 1997 to 1998, he was a visiting scholar with Bell Labs, Lucent Technologies. He is currently a Professor at the Tokyo Institute of Technology. His research interests include speech recognition, video information retrieval, and human interfaces.

Wikification and Beyond: The Challenges of Entity and Concept Grounding

Dan Roth
University of Illinois at Urbana-Champaign
danr@illinois.edu

Heng Ji
Rensselaer Polytechnic Institute
jih@rpi.edu

Ming-Wei Chang
Microsoft Research
minchang@microsoft.com

Taylor Cassidy
Army Research Lab & IBM Research
taylor.cassidy.ctr@mail.mil

1 Introduction

Contextual disambiguation and grounding of concepts and entities in natural language are essential to progress in many natural language understanding tasks and fundamental to many applications. Wikification aims at automatically identifying concept mentions in text and linking them to referents in a knowledge base (KB) (e.g., Wikipedia). Consider the sentence, "*The* ***Times*** *report on* ***Blumenthal (D)*** *has the potential to fundamentally reshape the contest in* ***the Nutmeg State***.". A Wikifier should identify the key entities and concepts and map them to an encyclopedic resource (e.g., "*D*" refers to *Democratic Party*, and "*the Nutmeg State*" refers to *Connecticut*.

Wikification benefits end-users and Natural Language Processing (NLP) systems. Readers can better comprehend Wikified documents as information about related topics is readily accessible. For systems, a Wikified document elucidates concepts and entities by grounding them in an encyclopedic resource or an ontology. Wikification output has improved NLP down-stream tasks, including coreference resolution, user interest discovery , recommendation and search.

This task has received increased attention in recent years from the NLP and Data Mining communities, partly fostered by the U.S. NIST Text Analysis Conference Knowledge Base Population (KBP) track, and several versions of it has been studied. These include Wikifying all concept mentions in a single text document; Wikifying a cluster of co-referential named entity mentions that appear across documents (Entity Linking), and Wikifying a whole document to a single concept. Other works relate this task to coreference resolution within and across documents and in the context of multiple text genres.

2 Content Overview

This tutorial will motivate Wikification as a broad paradigm for cross-source linking for knowledge enrichment. We will discuss multiple dimensions of the task definition, present the building blocks of a state-of-the-art Wikifier, share key lessons learned from analysis of results, and discuss recently proposed ideas for advancing work in this area in response to key challenges. We will touch on new research areas including interactive Wikification, social media, and censorship. The tutorial will be useful for all those with interests in cross-source information extraction and linking, knowledge acquisition, and the use of acquired knowledge in NLP. We will provide a concise roadmap of recent perspectives and results, and point to some of our available Wikification resources.

3 Outline

- Introduction and Motivation
- Methodological presentation of a skeletal Wikification system
  - Mention and candidate identification
  - Knowledge representation
  - Local and global context analysis
  - Role of Machine Learning
- Obstacles & Advanced Methods
  - Joint modeling
  - Collective inference
  - Scarcity of supervision signals
  - Diverse text genres and social media
- Remaining Challenges and Future Work
  - Rich semantic knowledge acquisition
  - Cross-lingual Wikification

References

http://nlp.cs.rpi.edu/kbp/2014/elreading.html

New Directions in Vector Space Models of Meaning

Phil Blunsom, Edward Grefenstette and Karl Moritz Hermann*
University of Oxford
first.last@cs.ox.ac.uk

Georgiana Dinu
Center for Mind/Brain Sciences
University of Trento
georgiana.dinu@unitn.it

1 Abstract

Symbolic approaches have dominated NLP as a means to model syntactic and semantic aspects of natural language. While powerful inferential tools exist for such models, they suffer from an inability to capture correlation between words and to provide a continuous model for word, phrase, and document similarity. Distributed representations are one mechanism to overcome these constraints.

This tutorial will supply NLP researchers with the mathematical and conceptual background to make use of vector-based models of meaning in their own research. We will begin by motivating the need for a transition from symbolic representations to distributed ones. We will briefly cover how collocational (distributional) vectors can be used and manipulated to model word meaning. We will discuss the progress from distributional to distributed representations, and how neural networks allow us to learn word vectors and condition them on metadata such as parallel texts, topic labels, or sentiment labels. Finally, we will present various forms of semantic vector composition, and discuss their relative strengths and weaknesses, and their application to problems such as language modelling, paraphrasing, machine translation and document classification.

This tutorial aims to bring researchers up to speed with recent developments in this fast-moving field. It aims to strike a balance between providing a general introduction to vector-based models of meaning, an analysis of diverging strands of research in the field, and also being a hands-on tutorial to equip NLP researchers with the necessary tools and background knowledge to start working on such models. Attendees should be comfortable with basic probability, linear algebra, and continuous mathematics. No substantial knowledge of machine learning is required.

*Instructors listed in alphabetical order.

2 Outline

1. Motivation: Meaning in space
2. Learning distributional models for words
3. Neural language modelling and distributed representations
   (a) Neural language model fundamentals
   (b) Recurrent neural language models
   (c) Conditional neural language models
4. Semantic composition in vector spaces
   (a) Algebraic and tensor-based composition
   (b) The role of non-linearities
   (c) Learning recursive neural models
   (d) Convolutional maps and composition

3 Instructors

Phil Blunsom is an Associate Professor at the University of Oxford's Department of Computer Science. His research centres on the probabilistic modelling of natural languages, with a particular interest in automating the discovery of structure and meaning in text.

Georgiana Dinu is a postdoctoral researcher at the University of Trento. Her research revolves around distributional semantics with a focus on compositionality within the distributional paradigm.

Edward Grefenstette is a postdoctoral researcher at Oxford's Department of Computer Science. He works on the relation between vector representations of language meaning and structured logical reasoning. His work in this area was recently recognised by a best paper award at *SEM 2013.

Karl Moritz Hermann is a final-year DPhil student at the Department of Computer Science in Oxford. His research studies distributed and compositional semantics, with a particular emphasis on mechanisms to reduce task-specific and monolingual syntactic bias in such representations.

Structured Belief Propagation for NLP

Matthew R. Gormley   **Jason Eisner**
Department of Computer Science
Johns Hopkins University, Baltimore, MD
{mrg, jason}@cs.jhu.edu

1 Tutorial Overview

Statistical natural language processing relies on probabilistic models of linguistic structure. More complex models can help capture our intuitions about language, by adding linguistically meaningful interactions and latent variables. However, inference and learning in the models we *want* often poses a serious computational challenge.

Belief propagation (BP) and its variants provide an attractive approximate solution, especially using recent training methods. These approaches can handle joint models of interacting components, are computationally efficient, and have extended the state-of-the-art on a number of common NLP tasks, including dependency parsing, modeling of morphological paradigms, CCG parsing, phrase extraction, semantic role labeling, and information extraction (Smith and Eisner, 2008; Dreyer and Eisner, 2009; Auli and Lopez, 2011; Burkett and Klein, 2012; Naradowsky et al., 2012; Stoyanov and Eisner, 2012).

This tutorial delves into BP with an emphasis on recent advances that enable state-of-the-art performance in a variety of tasks. Our goal is to elucidate how these approaches can easily be applied to new problems. We also cover the theory underlying them. Our target audience is researchers in human language technologies; we do not assume familarity with BP.

In the first three sections, we discuss applications of BP to NLP problems, the basics of modeling with factor graphs and message passing, and the theoretical underpinnings of "what BP is doing" and how it relates to other variational inference techniques. In the second three sections, we cover key extensions to the standard BP algorithm to enable modeling of linguistic structure, efficient inference, and approximation-aware training. We survey a variety of software tools and introduce a new software framework that incorporates many of the modern approaches covered in this tutorial.

2 Outline

1. Applications [15 min., Eisner]
   - Intro: Modeling with factor graphs
   - Morphological paradigms
   - Dependency and constituency parsing
   - Alignment; Phrase extraction
   - Relation extraction; Semantic role labeling
   - Targeted sentiment
   - Joint models for NLP
2. Belief Propagation Basics [40 min., Eisner]
   - Messages and beliefs
   - Sum-product, max-product, and deterministic annealing
   - Relation to forward-backward and inside-outside
   - Acyclic vs. loopy graphs
   - Synchronous vs. asynchronous propagation
3. Theory [25 min., Gormley]
   - From arc consistency to BP
   - From Gibbs sampling to particle BP to BP
   - Other message-passing algorithms
   - Bethe free energy
   - Connection to PFCGs and FSMs
4. Incorporating Structure into Factors and Variables [30 min., Gormley]
   - Embedding dynamic programs (e.g. inside-outside) within factors
   - String-valued and tree-valued variables
5. Message approximation and scheduling [20 min., Eisner]
   - Pruning messages
   - Variational approximations
   - Residual BP and new variants
6. Approximation-aware Training [30 min., Gormley]
   - Empirical risk minimization under approximations (ERMA)
   - BP as a computational expression graph
   - Automatic differentiation (AD)
7. Software [10 min., Gormley]

3 Instructors

Matt Gormley is a PhD student at Johns Hopkins University working with Mark Dredze and Jason Eisner. His current research focuses on joint modeling of multiple linguistic strata in learning settings where supervised resources are scarce. He has authored papers in a variety of areas including topic modeling, global optimization, semantic role labeling, and grammar induction.

Jason Eisner is an Associate Professor in Computer Science and Cognitive Science at Johns Hopkins University, where he has received two school-wide awards for excellence in teaching. His 80+ papers have presented many models and algorithms spanning numerous areas of NLP. His goal is to develop the probabilistic modeling, inference, and learning techniques needed for a unified model of all kinds of linguistic structure. In particular, he and his students introduced structured belief propagation, which integrates classical NLP models and their associated dynamic programming algorithms, as well as loss-calibrated training for use with belief propagation.

References

Michael Auli and Adam Lopez. 2011. A comparison of loopy belief propagation and dual decomposition for integrated CCG supertagging and parsing. In *Proceedings of ACL*.

David Burkett and Dan Klein. 2012. Fast inference in phrase extraction models with belief propagation. In *Proceedings of NAACL*.

Markus Dreyer and Jason Eisner. 2009. Graphical models over multiple strings. In *Proceedings of EMNLP*.

Jason Naradowsky, Sebastian Riedel, and David Smith. 2012. Improving NLP through marginalization of hidden syntactic structure. In *Proceedings of EMNLP 2012*.

David A. Smith and Jason Eisner. 2008. Dependency parsing by belief propagation. In *Proceedings of EMNLP*.

Veselin Stoyanov and Jason Eisner. 2012. Minimum-risk training of approximate CRF-Based NLP systems. In *Proceedings of NAACL-HLT*.

Semantics, Discourse and Statistical Machine Translation

Deyi Xiong and **Min Zhang**
Provincial Key Laboratory for Computer Information Processing Technology
Soochow University, Suzhou, China 215006
{dyxiong, minzhang}@suda.edu.cn

1 Description

In the past decade, statistical machine translation (SMT) has been advanced from word-based SMT to phrase- and syntax-based SMT. Although this advancement produces significant improvements in BLEU scores, crucial meaning errors and lack of cross-sentence connections at discourse level still hurt the quality of SMT-generated translations. More recently, we have witnessed two active movements in SMT research: one towards combining semantics and SMT in attempt to generate not only grammatical but also meaning-preserved translations, and the other towards exploring discourse knowledge for document-level machine translation in order to capture inter-sentence dependencies.

The emergence of semantic SMT are due to the combination of two factors: the necessity of semantic modeling in SMT and the renewed interest of designing models tailored to relevant NLP/SMT applications in the semantics community. The former is represented by recent numerous studies on exploring word sense disambiguation, semantic role labeling, bilingual semantic representations as well as semantic evaluation for SMT. The latter is reflected in CoNLL shared tasks, SemEval and SenEval exercises in recent years.

The need of capturing cross-sentence dependencies for document-level SMT triggers the resurgent interest of modeling translation from the perspective of discourse. Discourse phenomena, such as coherent relations, discourse topics, lexical cohesion that are beyond the scope of conventional sentence-level n-grams, have been recently considered and explored in the context of SMT.

This tutorial aims at providing a timely and combined introduction of such recent work along these two trends as discourse is inherently connected with semantics. The tutorial has three parts. The first part critically reviews the phrase- and syntax-based SMT. The second part is devoted to the lines of research oriented to semantic SMT, including a brief introduction of semantics, lexical and shallow semantics tailored to SMT, semantic representations in SMT, semantically motivated evaluation as well as advanced topics on deep semantic learning for SMT. The third part is dedicated to recent work on SMT with discourse, including a brief review on discourse studies from linguistics and computational viewpoints, discourse research from monolingual to multilingual, discourse-based SMT and a few advanced topics.

The tutorial is targeted for researchers in the SMT, semantics and discourse communities. In particular, the expected audience comes from two groups: 1) Researchers and students in the SMT community who want to design cutting-edge models and algorithms for semantic SMT with various semantic knowledge and representations, and who would like to advance SMT from sentence-by-sentence translation to document-level translation with discourse information; 2) Researchers and students from the semantics and discourse community who are interested in developing models and methods and adapting them to SMT.

2 Outline

1. SMT Overall Review (30 minutes)
    - SMT architecture
    - phrase- and syntax-based SMT
2. Semantics and SMT (1 hour and 15 minutes)
    - Brief introduction of semantics
    - Lexical semantics for SMT
    - Semantic representations in SMT
    - Semantically Motivated Evaluation
    - Advanced topics: deep semantic learning for SMT
    - Future directions

3. Discourse and SMT (1 hour and 15 minutes)
   - Introduction of discourse: linguistics, computational and bilingual discourse
   - Discourse-based SMT: modeling, training, decoding and evaluation
   - Future directions

3 Bios of Presenters

Dr. Deyi Xiong is a professor at Sochoow University. His research interests are in the area of natural language processing, particularly statistical machine translation and parsing. Previously he was a research scientist at the Institute for Infocomm Research of Singapore. He received the B.Sc degree from China University of Geosciences (Wuhan, China) in 2002, the Ph.D.degree from the Institute of Computing Technology (Beijing, China) in 2007, both in computer science. He has published papers in prestigious journals and conferences on statistical machine translation, including Computational Linguistics, IEEE TASLP, JAIR, NLE, ACL, EMNLP, AAAI and IJCAI. He was the program co-chair of IALP 2012 and CLIA workshop 2011.

Dr. Min Zhang, a distinguished professor and Director of the Research Center of Human Language Technology at Soochow University (China), received his Bachelor degree and Ph.D. degree in computer science from Harbin Institute of Technology in 1991 and 1997, respectively. From 1997 to 1999, he worked as a postdoctoral research fellow in Korean Advanced Institute of Science and Technology in South Korea. He began his academic and industrial career as a researcher at Lernout & Hauspie Asia Pacific (Singapore) in Sep. 1999. He joined Infotalk Technology (Singapore) as a researcher in 2001 and became a senior research manager in 2002. He joined the Institute for Infocomm Research (Singapore) as a research scientist in Dec. 2003. He joined the Soochow University as a distinguished professor in 2012.

His current research interests include machine translation, natural language processing, information extraction, social network computing and Internet intelligence. He has co-authored more than 150 papers in leading journals and conferences, and co-edited 10 books/proceedings published by Springer and IEEE. He was the recipient of several awards in China and oversea. He is the vice president of COLIPS (2011-2013), the elected vice chair of SIGHAN/ACL (2014-2015), a steering committee member of PACLIC (2011-now), an executive member of AFNLP (2013-2014) and a member of ACL (since 2006). He supervises Ph.D students at National University of Singapore, Harbin Institute of Technology and Soochow University.

Incremental Structured Prediction Using a Global Learning and Beam-Search Framework

Yue Zhang[†], **Meishan Zhang**[‡], **Ting Liu**[‡]
[†]Singapore University of Technology and Design
yue_zhang@sutd.edu.sg
[‡]Research Center for Social Computing and Information Retrieval
Harbin Institute of Technology, China
{mszhang, tliu}@ir.hit.edu.cn

Abstract

This tutorial discusses a framework for incremental left-to-right structured predication, which makes use of global discriminative learning and beam-search decoding. The method has been applied to a wide range of NLP tasks in recent years, and achieved competitive accuracies and efficiencies. We give an introduction to the algorithms and efficient implementations, and discuss their applications to a range of NLP tasks.

1 Introduction

This tutorial discusses a framework of online global discriminative learning and beam-search decoding for syntactic processing (Zhang and Clark, 2011b), which has recently been applied to a wide variety of natural language processing (NLP) tasks, including word segmentation (Zhang and Clark, 2007), dependency parsing (Zhang and Clark, 2008b; Huang and Sagae, 2010; Zhang and Nivre, 2011; Bohnet and Kuhn, 2012), context free grammar (CFG) parsing (Collins and Roark, 2004; Zhang and Clark, 2009; Zhu et al., 2013), combinational categorial grammar (CCG) parsing (Zhang and Clark, 2011a; Xu et al., 2014) and machine translation (Liu, 2013), achieving state-of-the-art accuracies and efficiencies. In addition, due to its high efficiencies, it has also been applied to a range of joint structural problems, such as joint segmentation and POS-tagging (Zhang and Clark, 2008a; Zhang and Clark, 2010), joint POS-tagging and dependency parsing (Hatori et al., 2011; Bohnet and Nivre, 2012), joint morphological analysis, POS-tagging and dependency parsing (Bohnet et al., 2013), and joint segmentation, POS-tagging and parsing (Zhang et al., 2013; Zhang et al., 2014).

In addition to the aforementioned tasks, the framework can be applied to all structural prediction tasks for which the output can be constructed using an incremental process. The advantage of this framework is two-fold. First, beam-search enables highly efficient decoding, which typically has linear time complexity, depending on the incremental process. Second, free from DP-style constraints and Markov-style independence assumptions, the framework allows arbitrary features to be defined to capture structural patterns. In addition to feature advantages, the high accuracies of this framework are also enabled by direct interactions between learning and search (Daumé III and Marcu, 2005; Huang et al., 2012; Zhang and Nivre, 2012).

2 Tutorial Overview

In this tutorial, we make an introduction to the framework, illustrating how it can be applied to a range of NLP problems, giving theoretical discussions and demonstrating a software implementation. We start with a detailed introduction of the framework, describing the averaged perceptron algorithm (Collins, 2002) and its efficient implementation issues (Zhang and Clark, 2007), as well as beam-search and the early-update strategy (Collins and Roark, 2004). We then illustrate how the framework can be applied to NLP tasks, including word segmentation, joint segmentation & POS-tagging, labeled and unlabeled dependency parsing, joint POS-tagging and dependency parsing, CFG parsing, CCG parsing, and joint segmentation, POS-tagging and parsing. In each case, we illustrate how the task is turned into an incremental left-to-right output-building process, and how rich features are defined to give competitive accuracies. These examples can serve as guidance in applying the framework to other structural prediction tasks.

In the second part of the tutorial, we give some analysis on why the framework is effective. We discuss several alternative learning algorithms, and compare beam-search with greedy search on dependency parsing. We show that accuracy benefits from interaction between learning and search. Finally, the tutorial concludes with an introduction to ZPar, an open source toolkit that provides optimized C++ implementations of of all the above tasks.

3 Outline

1 Introduction (0.5 hours)
  - 1.1 An overview of the syntactic processing framework and its applications
  - 1.2 An introduction to the beam-search framework and comparison to dynamic programming
  - 1.3 Algorithm in details
    - 1.3.1 Online discriminative learning using the perceptron
    - 1.3.2 Beam-search decoding
    - 1.3.3 The integrated framework

2 Applications (1.25 hours)
  - 2.1 Overview
  - 2.2 Word segmentation
  - 2.3 Joint segmentation and POS-tagging
  - 2.4 Dependency parsing
  - 2.5 Context free grammar parsing
  - 2.6 Combinatory categorial grammar parsing
  - 2.7 Joint segmentation, POS-tagging and parsing

3 Analysis of the framework (0.75 hours)
  - 3.1 The influence of global learning
  - 3.2 The influence of beam-search
  - 3.3 Benefits from the combination
  - 3.4 Related discussions

4 The ZPar software tool (0.5 hours)

4 About the Presenters

Yue Zhang is an Assistant Professor at Singapore University of Technology and Design (SUTD). Before joining SUTD in 2012, he worked as a postdoctoral research associate at University of Cambridge. He received his PhD and MSc degrees from University of Oxford, and undergraduate degree from Tsinghua University, China. Dr Zhang's research interest includes natural language parsing, natural language generation, machine translation and machine learning.

Meishan Zhang is a fifth-year Phd candidate at Research Center for Social Computing and Information Retrieval, Harbin Institute of Technology, China (HIT-SCIR). His research interest includes Chinese morphological and syntactic parsing, semantic representation and parsing, joint modelling and machine learning.

Ting Liu is a professor at HIT-SCIR. His research interest includes social computing, information retrieval and natural language processing.

References

Bernd Bohnet and Jonas Kuhn. 2012. The best of bothworlds – a graph-based completion model for transition-based parsers. In *Proceedings of EACL*, pages 77–87, Avignon, France, April. Association for Computational Linguistics.

Bernd Bohnet and Joakim Nivre. 2012. A transition-based system for joint part-of-speech tagging and labeled non-projective dependency parsing. In *Proceedings of EMNLP*, pages 1455–1465, Jeju Island, Korea, July. Association for Computational Linguistics.

Bernd Bohnet, Joakim Nivre, Igor Boguslavsky, Richard Farkas, Filip Ginter, and Jan Hajic. 2013. Joint morphological and syntactic analysis for richly inflected languages. *Transactions of the Association for Computational Linguistics*, 1:415–428.

Michael Collins and Brian Roark. 2004. Incremental parsing with the perceptron algorithm. In *Proceedings of ACL 2004, Main Volume*, pages 111–118, Barcelona, Spain, July.

Michael Collins. 2002. Discriminative training methods for hidden markov models: Theory and experiments with perceptron algorithms. In *Proceedings of EMNLP*, pages 1–8. Association for Computational Linguistics, July.

Hal Daumé III and Daniel Marcu. 2005. Learning as search optimization: Approximate large margin methods for structured prediction. In *International Conference on Machine Learning (ICML)*, Bonn, Germany.

Jun Hatori, Takuya Matsuzaki, Yusuke Miyao, and Jun'ichi Tsujii. 2011. Incremental joint pos tagging and dependency parsing in chinese. In *Proceedings of IJCNLP*, pages 1216–1224, Chiang Mai, Thailand, November. Asian Federation of Natural Language Processing.

Liang Huang and Kenji Sagae. 2010. Dynamic programming for linear-time incremental parsing. In *Proceedings of ACL 2010*, pages 1077–1086, Uppsala, Sweden, July. Association for Computational Linguistics.

Liang Huang, Suphan Fayong, and Yang Guo. 2012. Structured perceptron with inexact search. In *Proceedings of NAACL 2012*, pages 142–151, Montréal, Canada, June. Association for Computational Linguistics.

Yang Liu. 2013. A shift-reduce parsing algorithm for phrase-based string-to-dependency translation. In *Proceedings of the ACL*, pages 1–10, Sofia, Bulgaria, August. Association for Computational Linguistics.

Wenduan Xu, Yue Zhang, and Stephen Clark. 2014. Shift-reduce ccg parsing with a dependency model. In *Proceedings of the ACL*.

Yue Zhang and Stephen Clark. 2007. Chinese segmentation with a word-based perceptron algorithm. In *Proceedings of ACL 2007*, pages 840–847, Prague, Czech Republic, June. Association for Computational Linguistics.

Yue Zhang and Stephen Clark. 2008a. Joint word segmentation and POS tagging using a single perceptron. In *Proceedings of ACL-08: HLT*, pages 888–896, Columbus, Ohio, June. Association for Computational Linguistics.

Yue Zhang and Stephen Clark. 2008b. A tale of two parsers: Investigating and combining graph-based and transition-based dependency parsing. In *Proceedings of EMNLP*, pages 562–571, Honolulu, Hawaii, October. Association for Computational Linguistics.

Yue Zhang and Stephen Clark. 2009. Transition-based parsing of the chinese treebank using a global discriminative model. In *Proceedings of IWPT'09*, pages 162–171, Paris, France, October. Association for Computational Linguistics.

Yue Zhang and Stephen Clark. 2010. A fast decoder for joint word segmentation and POS-tagging using a single discriminative model. In *Proceedings of EMNLP 2010*, pages 843–852, Cambridge, MA, October. Association for Computational Linguistics.

Yue Zhang and Stephen Clark. 2011a. Shift-reduce ccg parsing. In *Proceedings of ACL 2011*, pages 683–692, Portland, Oregon, USA, June. Association for Computational Linguistics.

Yue Zhang and Stephen Clark. 2011b. Syntactic processing using the generalized perceptron and beam search. *Computational Linguistics*, 37(1):105–151.

Yue Zhang and Joakim Nivre. 2011. Transition-based dependency parsing with rich non-local features. In *Proceedings of ACL 2011*, pages 188–193, Portland, Oregon, USA, June. Association for Computational Linguistics.

Yue Zhang and Joakim Nivre. 2012. Analyzing the effect of global learning and beam-search on transition-based dependency parsing. In *Proceedings of COLING 2012: Posters*, pages 1391–1400, Mumbai, India, December. The COLING 2012 Organizing Committee.

Meishan Zhang, Yue Zhang, Wanxiang Che, and Ting Liu. 2013. Chinese parsing exploiting characters. In *Proceedings of ACL 2013*.

Meishan Zhang, Yue Zhang, Wanxiang Che, and Ting Liu. 2014. Character-level chinese dependency parsing. In *Proceedings of the ACL*.

Muhua Zhu, Yue Zhang, Wenliang Chen, Min Zhang, and Jingbo Zhu. 2013. Fast and accurate shift-reduce constituent parsing. In *Proceedings of ACL 2013*.

Author Index

Association for Computational Linguistics
209 N. Eighth Street
Stroudsburg, Pennsylvania 18360

proceedings
.com

Workshop on Natural Language Processing 2014

Held as part of the 5th Information Systems Research Working Days (JISIC 2014)

Quito, Ecuador
20 – 24 October 2014

ISBN: 978-1-63439-925-8